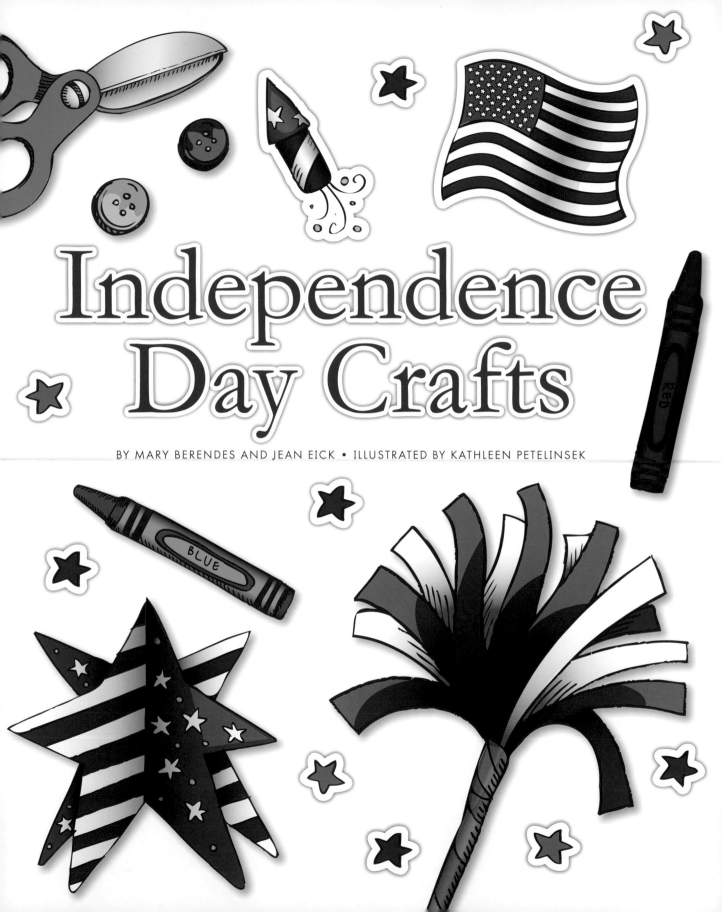

Independence Day Crafts

BY MARY BERENDES AND JEAN EICK • ILLUSTRATED BY KATHLEEN PETELINSEK

The
Child's
World®

Published by The Child's World®
1980 Lookout Drive
Mankato, MN 56003-1705
800-599-READ
www.childsworld.com

The Child's World®: Mary Berendes, Publishing Director
The Design Lab: Design and production

Library of Congress Cataloging-in-Publication Data
Berendes, Mary.
 Independence Day crafts / by Mary Berendes and Jean Eick;
illustrated by Kathleen Petelinsek.
    p. cm.
  ISBN 978-1-60954-235-1 (lib. bdg.: alk. paper)
1. Fourth of July decorations—Juvenile literature. 2. Handicraft—Juvenile
literature. I. Eick, Jean, 1947– II. Petelinsek, Kathleen, ill. III. Title.
TT900.F68B47 2011
745.594'1634—dc22   2010035482

Printed in the United States of America
Mankato, MN
December, 2010
PA02071

Table of Contents

It's Independence Day!

Independence Day is a special **holiday** for people in the United States. It is always **celebrated** on July 4. On this day, Americans celebrate our country's beginnings. They celebrate our country's ideas of freedom and bravery, too. It's a day to be proud of the United States.

People have celebrated Independence Day since 1776—that's over 200 years! It's a time to be with family and friends. Many cities and towns have parades. Families like to have barbecues and picnics. At the end of every Independence Day, Americans set off **fireworks**. The night sky is filled with bright colors and sparkles!

Let's Begin!

1 This book is full of great ideas you can make to celebrate Independence Day. There are ideas for decorations, gifts, and cards. There are activities at the end of this book, too!

2 Before you start making any craft, be sure to read the **directions**. Make sure you look at the pictures too—they will help you understand what to do. Go through the list of things you'll need and get everything together. When you're ready, find a good place to work. Now you can begin making your crafts!

Standing Star

These great stars are fun to place all around.

THINGS YOU'LL NEED

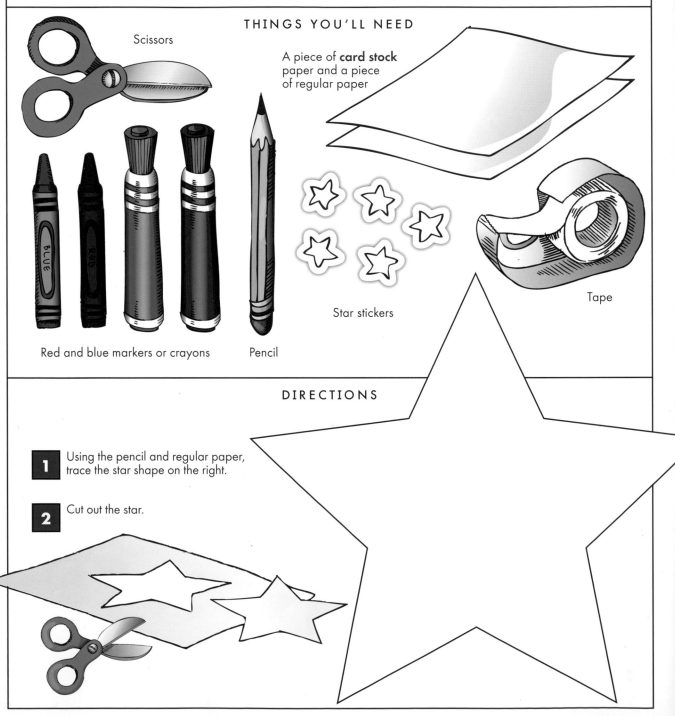

Scissors

A piece of **card stock** paper and a piece of regular paper

Star stickers

Tape

Red and blue markers or crayons

Pencil

DIRECTIONS

1 Using the pencil and regular paper, trace the star shape on the right.

2 Cut out the star.

3 Place the star on the card stock. Trace two of these star shapes on your card stock.

4 Use your scissors to cut out both stars.

5 On one star, draw red stripes.

6 Make a slit at the bottom of this star.

7 Color the other star blue.

8 Put lots of star stickers on the blue star.

9 Make a slit at the top of the blue star.

10 Place the red star's slit over the blue star's. Push down, and the slits will lock together.

11 Use some tape to stick the stars together a little more if you think your star is wobbly.

July 4th Wavers

These fun wavers are great to shake and wave in the wind.

THINGS YOU'LL NEED

Scissors

Ruler

Stapler

Stick (about 8 inches long)

4 Plastic bags
(red and white ones are best!)

Blue tape

DIRECTIONS

1 Stack the plastic bags neatly on top of each other.

2 Staple the bags together at the bottom edge. About 4 staples should do.

3 Use your scissors to cut off the handles. Now you should have a neat edge.

4 Use your ruler and scissors to cut strips in the bags. Each strip should be 3/4 inches wide. Be sure to stop cutting when you are 1 inch away from the stapled edge!

5 Cover all of the stick with the blue tape.

6 Wrap the stapled end of the bags around the top of the stick. Use the blue tape to hold it on.

7 If you want, crinkle the strips by gently crunching them with your hands. Now you have a fun waver to shake in the air!

Glitter Stars

Hang these stars all around for some Independence-Day sparkle!

THINGS YOU'LL NEED

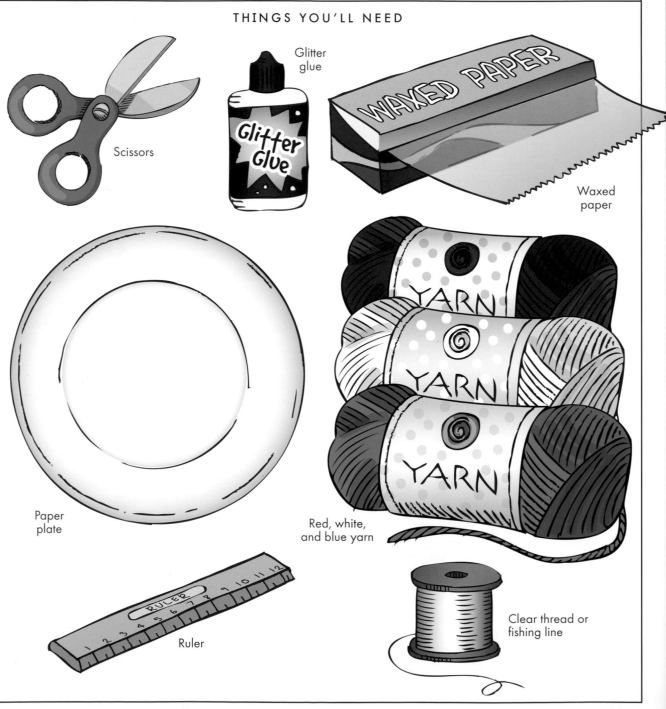

Scissors

Glitter glue

Waxed paper

Paper plate

Red, white, and blue yarn

Clear thread or fishing line

Ruler

DIRECTIONS

1 Place a large piece of waxed paper on a table or flat surface.

2 Use your ruler and scissors to make 5 strips of white yarn (each strip should be 3 inches long).

3 Do the same for the red yarn and blue yarn.

4 Squirt a large blob of the glitter glue onto the paper plate. Dip each piece of the white yarn in the glue. Cover it well!

5 Lay the glittery, gluey, white strips into a star shape on the wax paper. Be sure the ends of the yarn pieces are touching!

6 Do steps 4 and 5 for the red and blue yarn. You'll now have 1 white star, 1 red star, and 1 blue star. Let the stars dry for 1 day.

7 Very carefully peel the stars away from the waxed paper. Hang your stars using long pieces of the clear thread or fishing line.

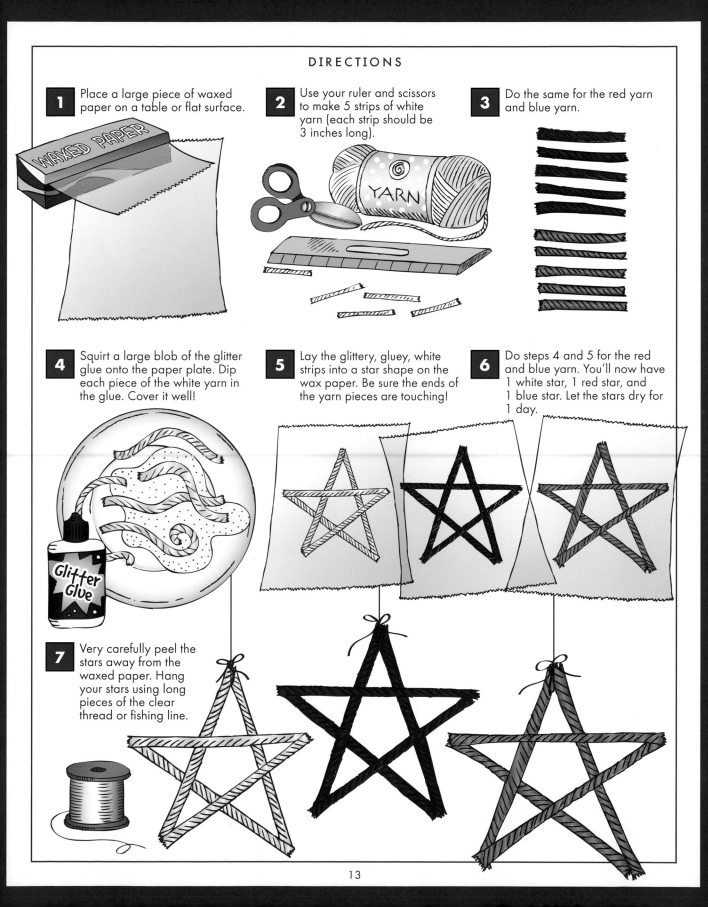

13

Flag Fans

This is a fun Independence-Day gift for any friend, parent, or teacher.

THINGS YOU'LL NEED

Scissors

Pencil

2 pieces of card stock
(1 white, 1 blue)

Glue

Red tape

2 paint stirring
sticks

Star stickers

Ruler

DIRECTIONS

1 Use your pencil and ruler to measure a square on each piece of card stock. The squares should be 8 inches long on each side.

2 Cut out each square.

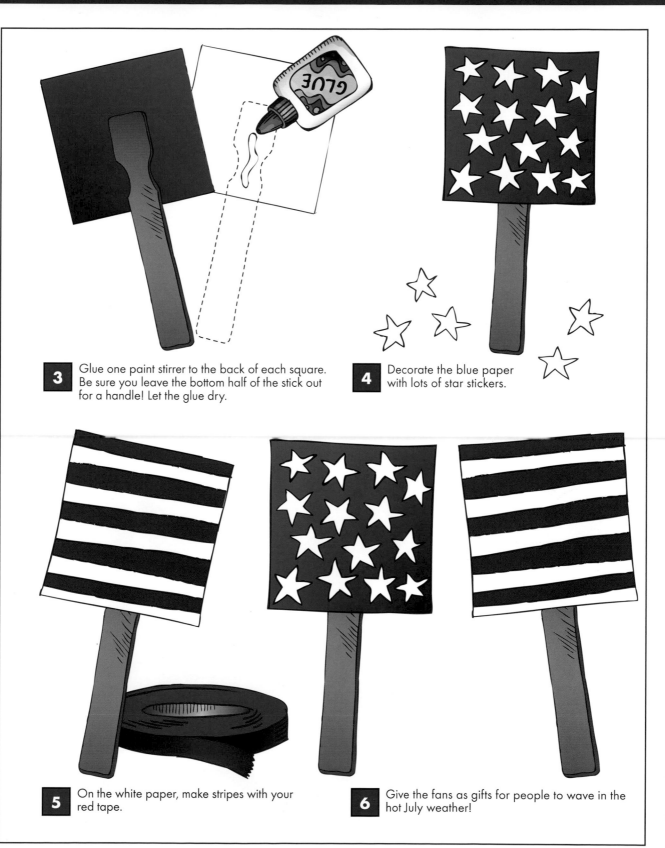

3 Glue one paint stirrer to the back of each square. Be sure you leave the bottom half of the stick out for a handle! Let the glue dry.

4 Decorate the blue paper with lots of star stickers.

5 On the white paper, make stripes with your red tape.

6 Give the fans as gifts for people to wave in the hot July weather!

Napkin Rings

These rings are great for holding napkins at a Fourth-of-July picnic.

THINGS YOU'LL NEED

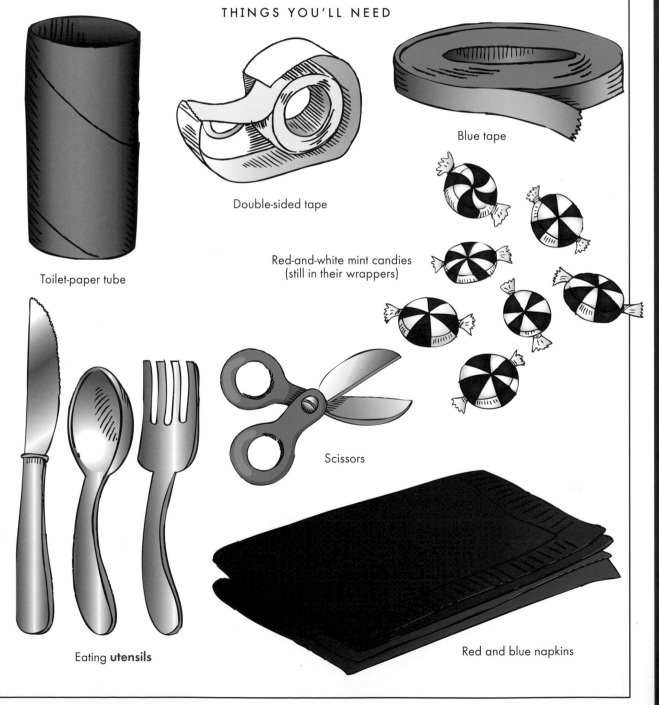

Toilet-paper tube

Double-sided tape

Blue tape

Red-and-white mint candies
(still in their wrappers)

Scissors

Eating **utensils**

Red and blue napkins

DIRECTIONS

1 Use your scissors to cut the tube in half. You now have two smaller tubes.

2 Cover each tube with the blue tape.

3 Use the double-sided tape to stick the wrapped mints all around each ring.

4 Place a napkin and one set of utensils inside each ring.

Cards

Giving cards is a very popular idea. You can send them to friends, teachers, and other special people.

THINGS YOU'LL NEED

Scissors

Construction paper (red, white, and blue is best)

Glitter

Glue

Ribbon

Buttons

Pencil

ORANGE YELLOW GREEN

BLUE

Crayons, markers, or paint

Stickers or magazine pictures

DIRECTIONS FOR CARD ONE

1 Fold a piece of construction paper to the size you want it to be. Folding once will make a large card. Folding it twice will make a smaller card.

2 Decorate the front of the card any way you'd like. You can use ribbons, buttons, glitter, and stickers. You can even use magazine pictures that remind you of the Fourth of July. Good ideas are flags, eagles, stars, and fireworks. Write a message on the inside of the card. You can decorate the inside, too. Don't forget to sign your name!

DIRECTIONS FOR CARD TWO

1 Instead of making a square card, make one shaped like a star! Use your pencil to draw a star shape on a folded piece of paper. Remember, the edge of the star must hang over the folded part of the paper!

2 Cut out the shape with your scissors.

3 Now open the card. You should see two stars!

4 Decorate the card however you'd like.

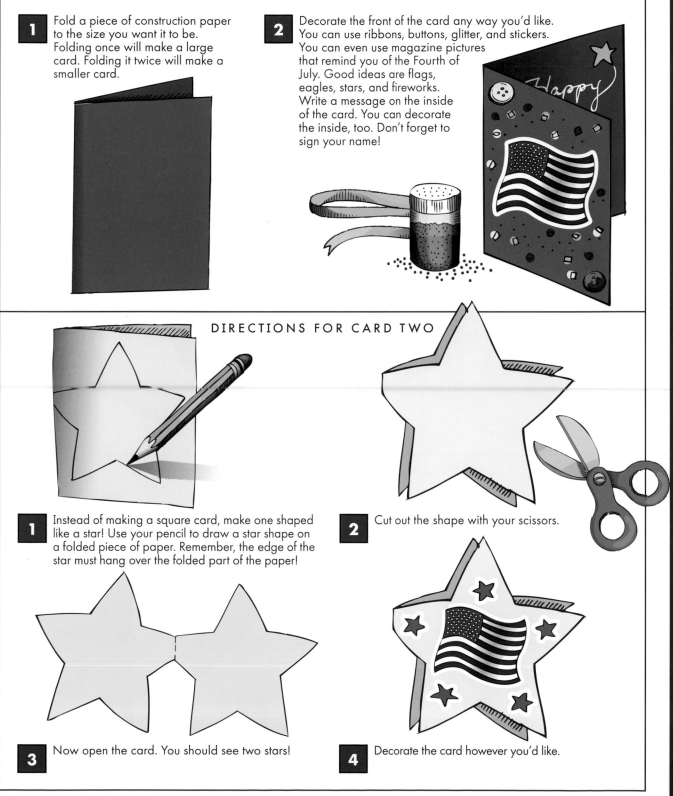

Envelopes

You can make your own envelopes to fit your homemade cards.

THINGS YOU'LL NEED

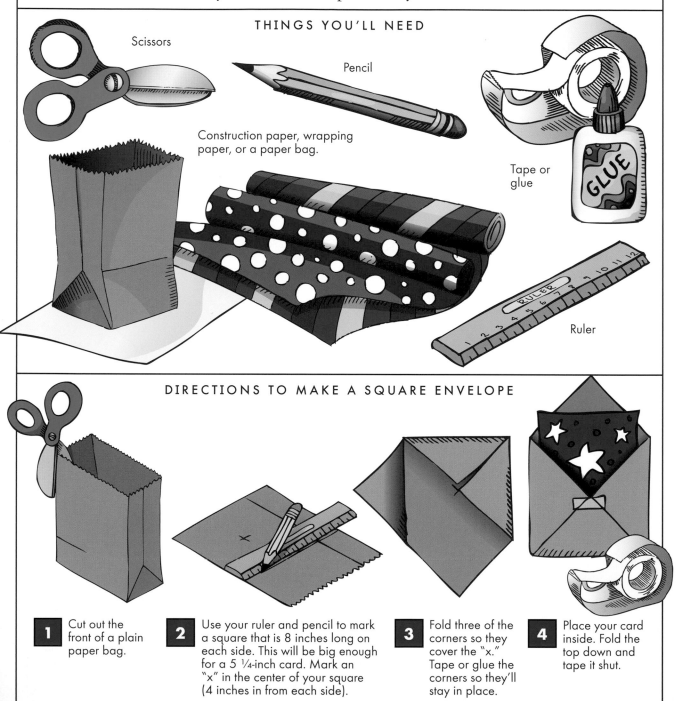

Scissors

Pencil

Construction paper, wrapping paper, or a paper bag.

Tape or glue

GLUE

RULER

Ruler

DIRECTIONS TO MAKE A SQUARE ENVELOPE

1 Cut out the front of a plain paper bag.

2 Use your ruler and pencil to mark a square that is 8 inches long on each side. This will be big enough for a 5 ¼-inch card. Mark an "x" in the center of your square (4 inches in from each side).

3 Fold three of the corners so they cover the "x." Tape or glue the corners so they'll stay in place.

4 Place your card inside. Fold the top down and tape it shut.

DIRECTIONS TO MAKE AN ENVELOPE THAT'S NOT SQUARE

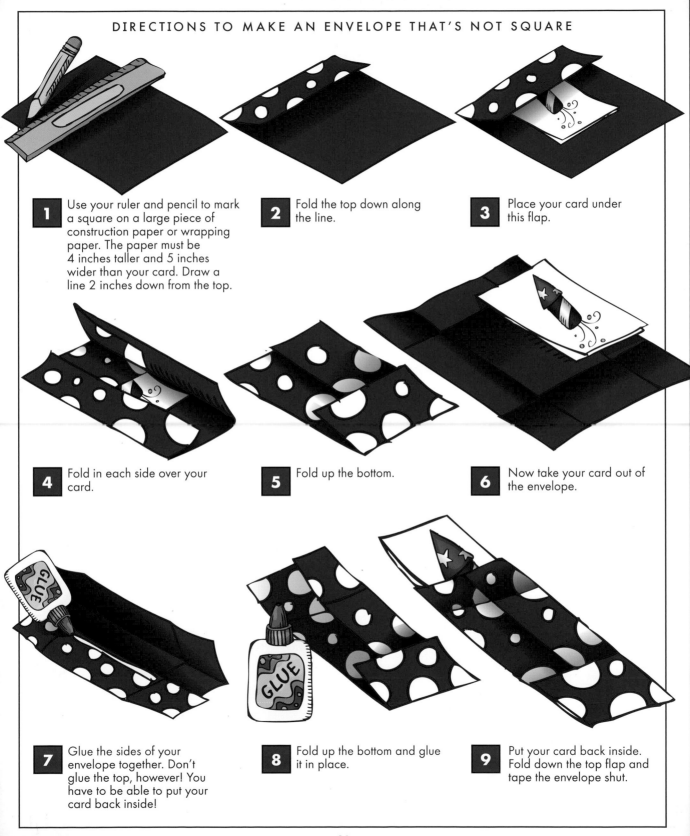

1 Use your ruler and pencil to mark a square on a large piece of construction paper or wrapping paper. The paper must be 4 inches taller and 5 inches wider than your card. Draw a line 2 inches down from the top.

2 Fold the top down along the line.

3 Place your card under this flap.

4 Fold in each side over your card.

5 Fold up the bottom.

6 Now take your card out of the envelope.

7 Glue the sides of your envelope together. Don't glue the top, however! You have to be able to put your card back inside!

8 Fold up the bottom and glue it in place.

9 Put your card back inside. Fold down the top flap and tape the envelope shut.

Activities

Independence Day is a fun time to do things with your family and friends. Here are some fun things to do together.

1 Chalk Art

Use lots of colorful chalk to draw pictures on your sidewalk or driveway that remind you of the Fourth of July. If there is a large group of people, some can be artists and others can vote on the best drawing.

2 Guess How Many

Have one person put wrapped red-and-white mint candies into a clear jar. That person should count how many candies they put in the jar—but not tell anyone else! Decorate the jar with a blue ribbon. Now pass the jar around. Everyone should guess how many candies are in the jar. The winner is the person who has the closest guess without going over.

3 Bike Parade

Independence Day is the perfect time for a parade! Have everyone decorate their bikes, skateboards, and scooters with red, white, and blue. Then have a parade for your friends and family!

Glossary

card stock (KARD STOK) Card stock is a very stiff kind of paper. It is useful in many crafts.

celebrated (SEL-uh-bray-ted) When people celebrate something, they do something happy and fun. Americans have celebrated Independence Day for over 200 years.

directions (dir-EK-shunz) Directions are the steps for how to do something. You should follow the directions in this book to make your crafts.

fireworks (FYR-wurks) Fireworks are special objects that explode into bright colors and flashes when they burn.

holiday (HOL-uh-day) A holiday is a time for celebration, such as Christmas or Valentine's Day. Independence Day is a holiday.

utensils (yoo-TEN-silz) Utensils are tools that are often used for cooking or eating. Knives, forks, and spoons are utensils.

Find More Crafts

BOOKS

Ross, Kathy, and Sharon Lane Holm (illustrator). *Star-Spangled Crafts*. Brookfield, CT: Millbrook Press, 2003.

Ross, Kathy, and Vicky Enright (illustrator). *Crafts to Make in the Summer*. Brookfield, CT: Millbrook Press, 1999.

WEB SITES

Visit our Web site for links to more crafts: childsworld.com/links

Note to Parents, Teachers, and Librarians: We routinely verify our Web links to make sure they are safe and active sites. So encourage your readers to check them out!

Index

ABOUT THE AUTHORS

Mary Berendes has authored dozens of books for children, including nature titles as well as books about countries and holidays. She loves to collect antique books and has some that are almost 200 years old. Mary lives in Minnesota.

Jean Eick has written over 200 books for children over the past forty years. She has written biographies, craft books, and many titles on nature and science. Jean lives in Lake Tahoe with her husband and enjoys hiking in the mountains, reading, and doing volunteer work.